My First Book
of
Memory Verses

Carine MacKenzie

CF4·K

Published by
Christian Focus Publications Ltd,
Geanies House, Fearn, Tain, Ross-shire,
IV20 1TW, Scotland, Great Britain.

www.christianfocus.com
email:info@christianfocus.com

Cover design by Alister MacInnes
Cover illustrations by Diane Mathes
Publication illustrations by Diane Mathes

Scripture taken from the New King James Version. Copyright © 1982 by Thomas Nelson, Inc. Used by permission. All rights reserved.

Printed and bound by Bell and Bain, Glasgow

Mixed Sources
Product group from well-managed
forests and other controlled sources
www.fsc.org Cert no. TT-COC-002769
© 1996 Forest Stewardship Council

From the Author

Memorising Scripture is a most valuable training for a child. Truths learned in youth stick with us and come back to our minds time and again. The Holy Spirit uses what we have learned and brings it back to our memory.

Jesus told his disciples "The Helper, the Holy Spirit, whom the Father will send in My name, he will teach you all things, and bring to your remembrance, all things that I have said to you." (John 14:26)

The Holy Spirit can only bring to our minds the things which we have already learned.

Encourage your children, not only to read God's word regularly, but to learn individual verses from it. This will prove to be a priceless treasure to them for all of their lives.

Carine MacKenzie

Contents

Genesis 1:1

In the beginning God created the heavens and the earth.

Everything in this universe was made by God.

He had no beginning and will have no end – He is eternal.

He is worthy of our praise and honour.

Isaiah 26:4

Trust in the Lord forever; for in the Lord JEHOVAH is everlasting strength.

God has power and great strength.

Because God is so strong we can safely trust in him.

Deuteronomy 33:27

The eternal God is your refuge, and underneath are the everlasting arms.

A refuge is a safe place to be. When a father wants to keep his little child safe, he puts his arms around him and underneath him. God is the best loving Father.

Numbers 6:24

The Lord bless you and keep you.

This prayer is that God would be kind and good to us and preserve us from all harm.

Lamentations 3:25

The Lord is good to those who wait for him, to the soul who seeks him.

God does not always answer our prayers immediately.

It is good for us to wait patiently for him and to realise that he does everything well and at the best time.

1 John 4:19

We love him (God), because he first loved us.

We know we love someone when we long to speak with them, we long to hear from them, we want to spend time with them.

We love God when we honour him, obey him, want to do what pleases him.

We can only do that because he has first loved us.

Genesis 16:13

You are the God who sees.

Sometimes we
do things and we
think that nobody
has seen us.

But God sees
everything we do.

He knows even our thoughts. This
should make a difference to the way
we behave.

Psalm 126:3

The Lord has done great things for us, whereof we are glad.

The list of great things God has done for us has no end.

We can try to count our blessings but we will not be able to tell of them all.

We can only say thank you.

Jesus

Isaiah 9:6

For unto a child is born, unto us a
Son is given: and the government
will be upon his shoulder. And his
name will be called Wonderful,
Counsellor, Mighty God, Everlasting
Father, Prince of Peace.

The birth of Jesus was foretold
hundreds of years
before it happened.
The prophet Isaiah
told about his mighty
power, wisdom and
care for his people.

Matthew 1:21

...You shall call his name Jesus, for he will save his people from their sins.

The name Jesus means 'Saviour'. The angel of the Lord appeared to Joseph in a dream and told him to call Mary's baby 'Jesus', because he would save his people from their sins – he would be the Saviour.

John 10:11

I am the good shepherd. The good shepherd gives his life for the sheep.

Jesus described himself as a good shepherd – one who would protect and guide and feed his flock of sheep – that is, the people who follow him. He gave his life for them.

John 14:6

Jesus said to him, "I am the way, the truth and the life. No one comes to the Father except through me."

The only way to God the Father is the Lord Jesus.

Jesus is the truth of God and the life of God.

John 6:35

And Jesus said to them, "I am the bread of life. He who comes to me shall never hunger, and he who believes in me shall never thirst."

Every person has a longing that needs to be satisfied.

This longing is like hunger or thirst.

The only satisfaction for this longing is in the Lord Jesus.

John 8:12

I am the light of the world. He who follows me shall not walk in darkness, but have the light of life.

If you were out walking in the countryside on a dark night, you would need a light to show you the way and to stop you from stumbling.

Jesus is the light to guide and help us in this dark sinful world.

Job 19:25

For I know that my Redeemer lives, and he shall stand at last on the earth.

Job wrote these words when he was suffering very badly.

He had hope and comfort in knowing that God, the redeemer, would do justly at the last day.

Psalm 23:1

The Lord is my shepherd; I shall not want.

The good shepherd takes care of his sheep.

He leads them to good pastures for food and quiet waters for drink.

God takes care of his people too – giving them food for body and for soul.

Mark 1:11

Then a voice came from heaven, "You are my beloved Son, in whom I am well pleased."

After Jesus, God the Son, was baptised, God the Holy Spirit came down on him like a dove, and God the Father spoke these words from heaven.

Romans 5:6

For when we were still without strength, in due time Christ died for the ungodly.

Jesus Christ died for his people – those who were weak and sinful.

This is the good news of the gospel.

Sin

John 1:29

Behold! The Lamb of God, who takes away the sin of the world!

John spoke these words when he saw Jesus coming towards him.

They would remind the people of the lamb that was used in sacrifice.

This gave a hint that Jesus would one day be offered as the sacrifice for sin.

Psalm 103:12

As far as the east is from the west, so far has he removed our transgressions from us.

The distance between north and south can be measured between the North and South poles. But the distance between east and west can never be measured. When we travel west we can still go even further west. This is a picture of the immeasurable distance that God puts between us and our sins.

Romans 6:23

For the wages of sin is death, but the gift of God is eternal life in Christ Jesus our Lord.

Wages are earned. Death is what we earn or deserve because of our sin.

God does not give his people what they earn - he gives them the wonderful undeserved gift of eternal life because of the work of our Saviour, Jesus Christ.

Psalm 51:2

Wash me thoroughly from my iniquity, and cleanse me from my sin.

Sin makes our lives black and dirty in God's sight. Only he can wash us and make us clean – not with soap and water – but with the precious blood of Jesus shed for us on Calvary's cross.

Isaiah 1:18

"Come now, and let us reason together, says the Lord, though your sins are like scarlet, they shall be as white as snow, though they are red like crimson, they shall be as wool."

Our sins are described as being scarlet or crimson - bright red in colour. But God's promise of forgiveness is like the pure white snow and the soft white wool. What a contrast!

Luke 5:32

I have not come to call the righteous, but sinners, to repentance.

The people who think they are good, do not see their need of a Saviour. Those who know they are sinners are called to repent by God. To repent means to turn from sin and to be truly sorry for it.

Salvation

John 3:16

For God so loved the world that he gave his only begotten Son, that whoever believes in him should not perish but have everlasting life.

This verse sums up the good news

of the gospel. God gave the best gift – his only Son, Jesus. Whoever believes in him and trusts in what he has done, will have the privilege of everlasting life with him in heaven.

Romans 5:8

But God demonstrates his own love toward us, in that while we were still sinners, Christ died for us.

Christ died to save sinners. We must come to him as sinners. We do not have to prove that we are even a little bit good.
Christ has taken
our place.

Ephesians 2:8

For by grace you have been saved through faith, and that not of yourselves, it is the gift of God.

The gift of salvation from God comes to us by grace – we do not deserve it – we cannot pay him back. We receive it through faith – by trusting wholly in him.

Acts 4:12

Nor is there salvation in any other, for there is none other name under heaven given among men by which we must be saved.

Salvation comes only through Jesus. No other person can do what he did.

Isaiah 45:22

"Look to me, and be saved, all you ends of the earth! For I am God, and there is no other."

Jesus came to save people from every continent – people of all races and colours and languages.

 His followers are told to spread the good news to every part of the world.

Mark 5:36

Do not be afraid; only believe.

Jesus spoke these comforting words to Jairus when news came that his little girl had just died.

Jesus went to the house and restored the little girl to life.

Everyone who saw it was amazed.

Habakkuk 3:18

Yet I will rejoice in the Lord, I will joy in the God of my salvation.

When God gives his gift of salvation, it causes great joy in our hearts. This joy comes only from God.

Acts 16:31

Believe on the Lord Jesus Christ, and you will be saved, you and your household.

This was the answer Paul and Silas gave when a man asked "What must I do to be saved?" The important message for him and for all of his family was to BELIEVE on the Lord Jesus Christ. This is important for us too.

Prayer

Psalm 119:18

Open my eyes, that I may see wondrous things from your law.

Before we read the Bible, it is good to pray like this, asking God to give us the understanding to see the wonderful truths in his word.

Hebrews 4:16

Let us therefore come boldly to the throne of grace, that we may obtain mercy and find grace to help in time of need.

We should not be afraid to pray. Our loving, merciful God wants us to come to him. He gives mercy and

forgiveness to the repentant sinner and love and grace to the needy person.

1 Thessalonians 5:18

In everything give thanks; for this is the will of God in Christ Jesus for you.

Prayer is not just asking for God to supply our needs and sort out our problems. An important part of prayer is saying 'Thank you' for everything.

Matthew 7:7

Ask, and it will be given to you; seek, and you will find; knock, and it will be opened to you.

Jesus told us to come to God in prayer – to ask and to seek and to knock. God is  gracious and will answer our prayers, but not always in the way or at the time that we think best.

Philippians 4:6

Be anxious for nothing; but in everything by prayer and supplication, with thanksgiving, let you requests be made known to God.

No worry is too big to take to God. No worry is too small to take to God. We should tell him about everything remembering to be thankful for all his goodness.

Instructions

Philippians 4:4

Rejoice in the Lord always. Again I will say, rejoice!

When we remember what God has done for us and is still doing for us everyday, we have good reason to be joyful.

Isaiah 55:6

Seek the Lord while he may be found, call upon him while he is near.

God invites us to seek him and to pray to him for salvation. We should not put this off until a later date as that may be too late. The best time is NOW.

Ecclesiastes 12:1

Remember now your Creator in the days of your youth.

Boys and girls are asked by God to remember him when they are young. We have to remember that God is our Creator. He made us and everything in the world.

Deuteronomy 6:5

You shall love the Lord your God with all your heart, with all your soul, and with all your strength.

The Lord God requires our complete love – we ought to love him most of all – with all of our heart, soul and strength.

Joshua 1:9

Be strong and of good courage; do not be afraid, nor be dismayed, for the Lord your God is with you wherever you go.

God spoke these words to Joshua. We can believe them too. If God is with us, we need never be afraid.

Mark 10:14

Let the little children to come to me, and do not forbid them; for of such is the kingdom of God.

Jesus told his disciples to allow the little children to come to him. They were not to turn them away. Jesus still wants little children to come to him.

Acts 3:19

Repent therefore and be converted, that your sins may be blotted out, so that times of refreshing may come from the presence of the Lord.

To repent means to be truly sorry for our evil thoughts and words and actions. We want to stop sinning and to live to please God.

Faith

Galatians 5:22-23

But the fruit of the Spirit is love, joy, peace, longsuffering, kindness, goodness, faithfulness, gentleness, self-control.

If God the Holy Spirit is guiding you, faith will be shown in your life along with the other fruit of the Spirit.

Hebrews 11:1

Now faith is the substance of things hoped for, the evidence of things not seen.

Faith is a gift from God, when we trust him completely and believe what he tells us in his Word.

Psalm 56:11

In God I have put my trust: I will not be afraid. What can man do to me?

When we trust in God, we do not need to be afraid of what others will do to us or say about us.

Philippians 4:11

I have learned in whatsoever state
I am, to be content.

God provides all our needs. It is best
not to be envious of what others
have but to be content or happy with
what God has
given us. Paul
had learned
this.

1 Corinthians 13:13

And now abide faith, hope, love, these three; but the greatest of these is love.

Faith is a wonderful gift of God and so is hope. But the gift which will last throughout eternity is LOVE.

Promises

Genesis 8:22

While the earth remains, seedtime and harvest, cold and heat, winter and summer, and day and night shall not cease.

The seasons of the year, the weather, the darkness of the night and the light of the day are all under the control of God.

1 Peter 5:7

Casting all your care upon him; for he cares for you.

We should tell all our problems to God and ask him to help us. He loves and cares for us more than anyone else ever can.

Romans 8:28

And we know that all things work together for good to those who love God, to those who are the called according to his purpose.

The person who is called to follow God, and loves him, can be confident that all the experiences will have some good purpose.

Proverbs 8:17

I love those who love me; and those who seek me diligently will find me.

God's love is pure and true and everlasting. We can only love him in a weak and imperfect way. But he understands us. God wants us to love and serve him when we are young.

Nehemiah 8:10

The joy of the Lord is your strength.

Even when things are difficult, God gives his people a sense of peace and joy. This gives them the strength to go on and follow and trust him.

Matthew 11:28

Come to me, all you who labour and are heavy laden, and I will give you rest.

When we are in difficulty and feeling sad and troubled, the best place to go for comfort is to the Lord Jesus. He has promised to give us rest.

Revelation 3:20

Behold, I stand at the door and knock. If anyone hears my voice and opens the door, I will come in to him and dine with him, and he with me.

The Lord Jesus has promised friendship and fellowship to those who listen to him and accept him in their lives. If we refuse him we are foolish.

Mark 13:31

"Heaven and earth will pass away: but my words will by no means pass away."

The word of God will never be destroyed. Everything that we see around us will one day be gone. We ought to value and take heed to the Bible, God's Word.

Have you seen:

My 1st Book of Questions and Answers
by Carine Mackenzie

Children always have questions about what it means to be a Christian. Do they need a long philosophical answer? Not always - and it is simple answers to deep questions that feature in this book.

If you have ever wanted to know how to explain the Christian faith to young children in bite-sized chunks, then 'My 1st Book of Questions & Answers' will be of great help to you. In 114 profound questions and answers, backed by scripture proofs, best selling author Carine Mackenzie provides an invaluable tool to get you started.

ISBN: 978-1-85792-570-8

CHRISTIAN FOCUS PUBLICATIONS

Christian Focus | Christian Heritage | CF4K | Mentor

Christian Focus Publications publishes books for adults and children under its four main imprints: Christian Focus, Christian Heritage, CF4K and Mentor. Our books reflect that God's word is reliable and Jesus is the way to know him, and live for ever with him.

Our children's publication list includes a Sunday school curriculum that covers pre-school to early teens; puzzle and activity books. We also publish personal and family devotional titles, biographies and inspirational stories that children will love.

If you are looking for quality Bible teaching for children then we have an excellent range of Bible story and age specific theological books.

From pre-school to teenage fiction, we have it covered!

Find us at our web page:
www.christianfocus.com

CF4·K
Because you're never too young to know Jesus